# CLEVELAND

## STORIES

Vol. II

Literary Cleveland
2515 N. Taylor Rd.
Cleveland, OH 44118
info@litcleveland.org
www.litcleveland.org

Book design by Matt Larsen
Edited by Matt Weinkam, Literary Cleveland

ISBN: 978-1-7345589-0-6

# Cleveland Stories, Vol. II

## Acknowledgments
## Introduction

# Part I: What We Know

# Part II: What We Need

# Part III: What We Love

# Acknowledgments

Many thanks to Seeds of Literacy and especially Kara Krawiec for partnering with Literary Cleveland on this Cleveland Stories program. Thanks also to the instructors Charlotte Morgan, Damien Ware and Kisha Nicole Foster (our project fellow) for their creativity and compassion in working with their students. In addition, much gratitude to Ella Thomas at the Thea Bowman Center for providing classroom space, and to Brian Meggitt and the Cleveland Public Library for providing vintage photographs of the Mt. Pleasant neighborhood which are included in this book. Matt Larsen graciously volunteered his time and talent to design this book--we are eternally grateful. Our thanks and gratitude to the St. Luke's Foundation for funding this project; it wouldn't exist without their generous support.

Any views, findings, conclusions or recommendations expressed in this program do not necessarily represent those of the St. Luke's Foundation, Literary Cleveland or other supporting organizations.

Kara Krawiec

# INTRODUCTION

Building on the success of last year, the 2019 Cleveland Stories project, organized by Literary Cleveland and funded in part by the St. Luke's Foundation, once again engaged with the residents of Mt. Pleasant and the surrounding neighborhoods. The goal: To further delve into the rich history of this area.

This is a place full of stories that, unfortunately, are not often heard—not because there is a lack of voices to tell them, but because Cleveland's east side is often seen as a place that no longer exists the way it once did. However, that is not Mt. Pleasant's only narrative. Its history is rich. Its story is grand. And those who live here know that there are more stories to be told.

Therefore, Literary Cleveland, in partnership with Seeds of Literacy, offered free writing workshops led by Charlotte Morgan, Kisha Nicole Foster, and DL Ware. In addition to the 27 poetry and prose pieces included in this anthology, there are also 28 photographs and reflections that further help paint an intricate portrait of the neighborhood as it once was, is now, and what it

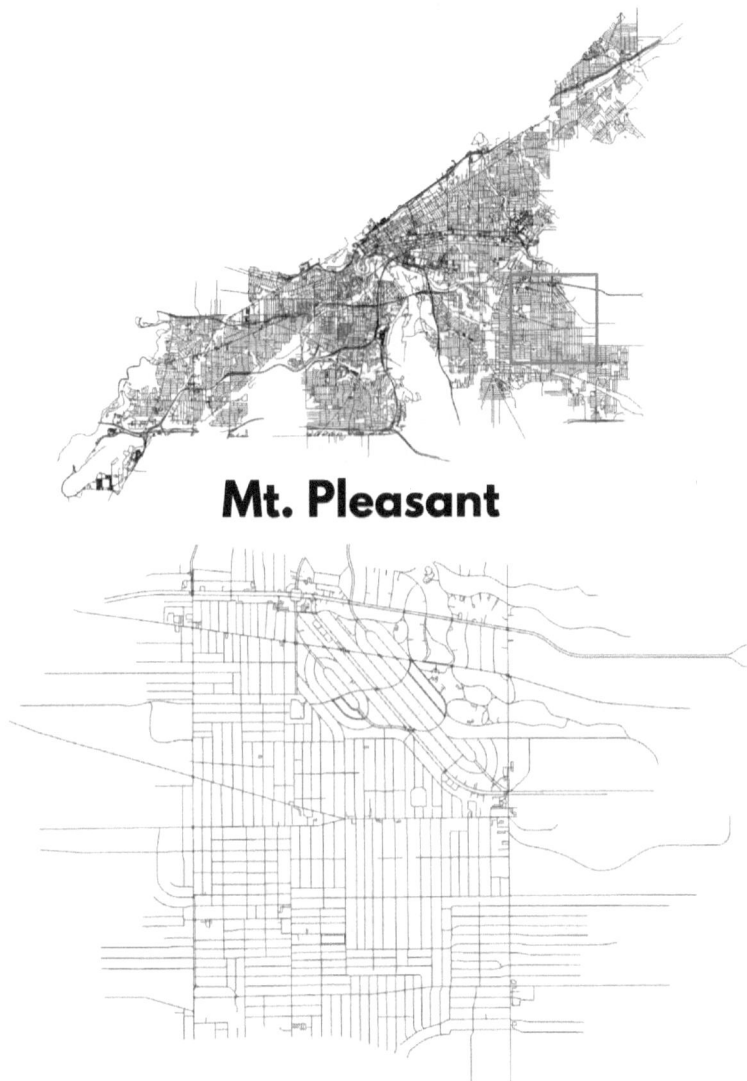

# Mt. Pleasant

can be in the future.

The work in this anthology is born out of a remarkable connection to place. The anthology itself weaves together a myriad of voices, allowing the reader to travel down the streets of Kinsman, Buckeye, Union, and Woodland through the eyes of those who have called this neighborhood home. These stories detail the struggle and strife as well as the striving and success of the Mt. Pleasant community in all its transformations.

Our contributors vividly tell readers what they know, what they need, and what they love about the Mt. Pleasant area. In her poem, "we are not these ruins," Danielle Dixon repeatedly urges her audience to think about the history of African Americans who survived and thrived in this neighborhood. Star Anderson, whose poem, "Why I Write," celebrates both the act and the necessity of writing, states that "I write cause sometimes / it's how I breathe."

These pieces also help bridge the gap between what Mt. Pleasant was and what modern day Mt. Pleasant is. This is exemplified in Lionel Johnson's "Friend," in which he recounts the story of his friend, Carl, against the backdrop of the shifting landscape of the neighborhood, highlighting the things that used to exist here.

Many of these contributors are also new writers who have found their voices in their craft. For instance, Rose Griffin ("The Family") has begun to blossom as a poet. She comes to class at Seeds of Literacy with a line on the tip of her tongue and by the end of the day she has a completed poem. Her piece, and many others, portray both the pain and joy that comes from our familial ties.

This anthology is a reminder that this community is not created from bricks and asphalt, but from the memories and voices of its residents, and the stories they share.

Kara Krawiec

Site Coordinator

Seeds of Literacy/East

# Part I: What We Know

Lionel Johnson

# Reflection:
# E. 130th & Kinsman

---

I remember the L.T. Huff Realty company at 130th and Kinsman. I was told that L.T. Huff Sr. started the company years before I came to the area. By that time, L.T. Huff Jr. and his mother were running the company. L.T. was a sharp dresser, as a lot of people were in those days. Dressing up is something that has been lost. L.T. would dress up and park his shiny new Cadillac in front of the real estate company. His car was always new. He must have always gotten a new car every year or two. This was before leasing became popular. He would get out of his car wearing a fancy suit with nice shoes, usually alligator shoes or some other kind of reptile like snake or lizard. I was a young teenager then. I aspired to dress that same way. I would go downtown with the little money that I had to buy the same kind of shoes or suit—a fancy casual outfit of dress pants and a fine Italian shirt. My friends did the same. Everyone was not dressed up in those days, but my friends and I tried to be dressed up everytime we came out of the pad. Kinsman Avenue was a bustling street of commerce back then. Across from L.T. Huff Realty was Brownies Bail Bonds office. That's where you went when you were

trying to get someone out of jail. Then there was the Golden Voice record shop. The son of the then-owner of Golden Voice was Billy Davis, an aspiring singer. I wonder what happened to Billy Davis. Next to Golden Voice was the pool room. The owner of the pool room would always kick me out, saying I was too young to be in the place. I would shrug my shoulders and go down to the pool room on 118th and Kinsman passing all kinds of stores and restaurants on the way.

Charlotte Morgan

# The Tales of Kidd Funkadelic Began in Mt. Pleasant

During the Rock and Roll Hall of Fame rehearsals in the downtown Cleveland Renaissance Hotel ballroom that Tuesday afternoon, May 6, 1997, when Parliament Funkadelic was set to be inducted, there stood legendary guitarist Michael Hampton. I know because I was there watching and taking notes. Michael's solos on Parliament and Funkadelic classic hits like "(Not Just) Knee Deep" and "One Nation Under A Groove" had made him legendary. He helped the group move from music's underground to hall of fame status. The rock, funk, and soul outfit not only put on elaborate stage spectacles that rivaled rock bands, but they featured some of the world's most talented musicians and vocalists whose names you may not know.

Michael left Cleveland nearly 22 years earlier to join George Clinton's group. He was a 40-year-old man now and back home; his eyes were affixed on the stage as another Michael rehearsed. The astonishment and reverence on his face for Michael Jackson was clear. One can only wonder what the hometown guitarist was

thinking. Later, he said he thought about what he had gone through to earn his place in music history—all the touring, traveling, and recording.

-

As I began thinking about music and the Mt. Pleasant area, I remembered that one of Cleveland's most famous black guitar heroes' rise to fame had origins in a house off Kinsman Road. I contacted an old friend, Ed Sparks, a local musician. We talked on the phone and he visited me at Cleveland State to tell me the story about the night the legend of Kidd Funkadelic began.

-

Once upon a time in Cleveland, WMMS 100.7 FM on-air jock Billy Bass would play Funkadelics' 10-minute opus, "Maggot Brain" around 1:30 am Sunday morning—it was a ritual. The band's aesthetic during the early 1970s was strictly a sublime cosmic slop—meaning it was about the black power movement which emerged following the civil rights era and the death of Martin Luther King, Bobby Kennedy, and Malcolm X. The music featured acid stimulated lyrics that inspired psychedelic wonderment and life beyond the stars. When released in 1971, on Westbound Records, every kid who played guitar wanted to play Eddie Hazel's solos to show how good they were.

In 1974, when Michael Hampton, a baby-faced 17-year-old guitar prodigy from 12837 North Avenue on Cleveland's west side, performed a note-for-note rendition of the psychedelic anthem at an after party in the Mt. Pleasant living room of Ed Sparks' house at 3441 E. 119th off Kinsman, no one knew it would change music history and land the guitarist in the Rock and Roll Hall of Fame.

When asked about that fateful night, Hampton reminiscenced, "My cousin (Lige Curry) played bass. I had showed him the chords to "Maggot Brain" and we played it in the living room. The band was around me. I didn't know it was Eddie Hazel [guitarist] and [drummer] Tiki Fulwood—it was the whole band— Gary (Shider) and Boogie (Cordell Mosson). They were all there and they heard me play."

Bass player Sparks, the leader of the Elektrik Sparks Band, himself a local legend, takes credit for the kismet which landed the teenager in the one of music's most renown recording and tour acts, Parliament-Funkadelic.

"My cousin Norman Young had been telling me about this killer guitar player on the west side who was just blowing everybody away... So, I said, 'Sure I'd love to meet this guy. My cousin went and picked Michael up and brought him to my house off Kinsman and soon, Michael and I started the Elektrik Sparks Band".

The group played together for two years before that fateful night that changed both Michael and Ed's life. The date was June 23, 1974. Sparks, who had met George Clinton a few years earlier, invited the band back to his house to celebrate his birthday. However, in fact, it was the chance for Clinton to hear Hampton shred "Maggot Brain." Ed shared with me blurry and faded photos that document the night.

Sparks has recounted the important night millions of times—even to famed *Plain Dealer* reporter, Jane Scott. In a 1993 interview before Parliament Funkadelic played the Front Row Theater in Mayfield Heights, he fondly recalls in 1974 being invited backstage at the Agora Ballroom by concert promoter Louis Moore of Brick City Productions. "I had the nerve to ask George Clinton if I could come onstage and sing a song with the band. Afterwards, we partied backstage with the band."

Eventually, everyone winds up at Sparks' home on E. 119th off Kinsman. According to Sparks, "When guitarist Eddie Hazel was arrested two weeks later, Gary Shider, the band director, phoned Cleveland to see if the kid was available. Next, Michael found himself onstage in Maryland performing "Maggot Brain"—the tale of Kidd Funkadelic had begun.

Hampton recalled, "I did my first show in Landover, Maryland, at this place called the Capital Centre—now it's a mall—but that was the first place that had closed-circuit TV sync. I looked up and I started off the set—it was sold out. I played 'Maggot Brain'—that was all I used to play."

Soon, Michael's solo became the high point in a three-and-a-half-hour show that was at times a rock opera that featured costumed musicians, singers, and props. I was a teenager attending a concert on an Easter Sunday when I first saw Kidd Funkadelic perform at the downtown Allen Theater. With his head down, he merged with his instrument on hits like "Cosmic Slop" and "Mothership Connection"—I realized I had never seen nor heard anything like before. I became a fan.

When I began working as a music journalist at *Scene Magazine*, I covered Parliament-Funkadelic, a two-headed music group with distinct personalities—one psychedelic rock, which featured Michael Hampton's lead guitar and Parliament, which featured a wall of vocals and funky bass, keyboards, and drums, accented by sassy horns. "The Clones of Dr. Funkenstein" was a piece that earned the cover of the regional publication and starred a toy Kidd Funkadelic in the grasp of Dr. Funkenstein (aka George Clinton). I was scheduled to conduct an interview backstage at Public Hall for a feature with the Kidd, but he never appeared. Instead, I talked with his old bandmate, Ed Sparks who I met backstage. He instantly told me about his connection to Michael and the funk mob. We became friends. He threw a New Year's Eve house party in Glenville and invited me. I arrived to find Kidd Funkadelic sitting on some pillows in a corner by himself smoking a joint and drinking a beer.

While traveling to cover his band, my relationship grew. We'd see one another backstage in different cities, and he'd always greet me. Michael, who was very shy, learned to trust me. Eventually, I was invited to visit his family's home on North Avenue. My friends and I would spend hours in his room watching him drink beer and practice guitar riffs to a click track—a bare bones recording with no vocals just drums and perhaps a bass line. Michael would reach in a dresser drawer and pull out a random unmarked cassette, pop it in the player and jam to it. I heard riffs that would later wind up on subsequent P-funk recordings.

The walls leading up to the second floor were lined with gold and platinum albums that Michael had earned. His guitar solo on "(Not Just) Knee Deep," "One Nation Under A Groove," as well as the epic one on the Brides of Funkenstein's 15-minutes track, "Never Buy Texas From A Cowboy," have become a part of the black music lexicon. Rolling Stone Magazine recognized that Brides LP as one of the Top 50 Coolest Albums. Journalists acknowledge that it was Kidd Funkadelic's solo that helped the recording become legendary.

He recalls, "For one solo, I was outside the booth (at United Sound Suite in Detroit) and the amp was isolated in the vocal booth. For the "(Not Just) Knee Deep" solo, I think it was a Fender Twin cranked all the way up. They had those microphones that stuck to the glass. But in order to get that sound, they isolated the amp. I was using my Alembic guitar, I forget what the model was, and there was a Morley wah and I think they had a Marshall stack. I was basically right next to the stack when I did that solo. I prefer to be right next to it, for feedback and other effects."

Michael said when he was in high school, his teacher took the whole class to see the symphony orchestra. "I was fortunate enough to check that out, and something about it just set something off—when I hear certain songs and the way they use the modes. I'm looking for what it makes me feel like, you know? Like wonderment. I'm trying to paint a feeling of whatever feeling I have."

His unique style has often put him in the same category as a Jimi Hendrix, but he still remains unknown to today's young music fans. He says that what he does well is to try to put solos in there like how a drummer does a roll. George told him to play R&B. He plays a drum roll and sets it up for the melody. I'm always listening for that resolution. I might wander around in some different modes or scales, but I'm interested in trying to resolve it right on, at a time where people should understand it. It could be a slow or fast lead, but whatever it is should be resolved. "Oh, here it comes right here. Okay. And bring it back home."

-

On the night he returned to Cleveland to take his place in the Rock Hall, his brother Wade threw him a party up the street at the Wyndham Hotel. When I arrived at the rehearsal, Michael wasn't there. But as Michael Jackson began running through his dance moves, the room quieted, and I turned to see Kidd Funkadelic and Prince along the back wall staring at the stage. The Kidd was now hanging with other legends. During the induction ceremony, dressed in a suit, he took the stage with the P-Funk mob, his hair long hair braided—he still had that youthful look I remembered. When time for his speech came, he declared, "I'm from here. From the west side of Cleveland, and if it wasn't for "Maggot Brain" I wouldn't be here." He looked happy.

But the man known in the music industry as Kidd Funkadelic didn't mention those days and nights in that house off Kinsman Road and how his friend Ed Sparks' birthday party led to a gig in the iconic band, Parliament-Funkadelic.

Later, I spoke to Ed who had long since moved from the Mt. Pleasant home on E. 119th Street. "I'm so glad that I was able to bring Michael to George Clinton. And his cousin Lige Curry joined the band and now plays bass now. And there are times when he and his cousin are in town that they come by the house and we play together like in the old Elektrik Sparks days. They have even done a show or two with us."

The house is now gone, but the connection to music history remains.

*Ed Sparks died December 6, 2019. His role in music history and in the Mt. Pleasant neighborhood will not be forgotten.*

D.L. Ware

# Heavy Clouds Over South East Cleveland Remind Me of Gunmetal Grey

Grey clouds over the
South East remind me
that these Streets
have nothing to offer.

Nothing to offer but the
type of grief that
conjures sacred spirits
living in the names of
clouds that hover
over us, keeps their
memory alive,
in my mind a time when
we played as children.
        Douglas Clements. Rayshawn D.
        Armstrong. Jeffery Young.
Theses streets
pave the way,
like a stairway

to heaven, Gangstas
die early or be gone for long,
grown out the past,
into the future of
an early grave, often times
for nothing.
So my frustration is too
familiar with the violence
that consumes
the spaces between
my block, that alley, these streets,
and every goddamned corner.

So many have given their very lives
to walk these streets -
                93rd. Martin Luther King. 131st. 116th.
bound to the corners
as the prey
of invisible hands.
So many risk their lives to walk these streets
                Buckeye. Woodland. Kinsman. Union Ave.
Praying for their loved ones
And a safe return home.

Naima Omar

# A Walk Taken Many Times

Some things are still there but others are long gone and hard to picture. There are a few nice plots of grass where eyesores that were once homes and businesses stood for decades. It's a miracle that no one fell into the basement of that one old apartment building before it was removed from the earth. The building next to it that used to have a check cashing place is undergoing a tedious transformation with a few bricks being removed daily.

Long ago it was Dairy Mart then it became Mister V's. Verdell has long since passed on along with the ability to open the store at consistent times and get the coolers fixed. I don't know why they still hold on to it, maybe just to honor his memory.

As a child I would sometimes purchase pickles from Native Son by my maternal grandmother used the place for its intended purpose, to hang out and listen to music. Now it's a Whitmores that still attracts a party crowd.

At some point in history there was a Rite Aid on almost every corner. That era didn't last and they both became day care centers.

I've seen people getting haircuts at 6am I have no idea how long that has been going on.

When we used to watch *Fat Albert*, we would imagine it took place in our neighborhood because we had a hardware store in common. I don't ever remember actually going in that hardware store; seems like it's always been abandoned.

There was a conveniently located clinic that gave way to day care and eventually nothingness.

I remember playing video games at one corner store or another. There were so many I don't know which was which.

The Catholic church was beautiful and foreign and full of white Jesus and his momma. It has a new life with a female minister.

There was a clothing store that I never got a chance to shop in before it switched to appliances.

A laundromat held on to the bitter end before the city finally put it out of its misery.

A garage perished along with it.

A Golden Light went out with a flame that destroyed

any evidence of its previous existence. It had a few neighbors that morphed and eventually passed with very little notice. At one point there was a thrift store with a restaurant next door.

Save Mor was reborn as Sav a Lot but my Dad still says they sell nigger food.

Sometimes I still can't believe McDonalds is dead, replaced by one of the top three most ubiquitous stores in the city. Rally's on the other had emerged from its coma years later as if nothing ever happened to it

Sometimes I still call it Society though it was bought by Key Bank long ago. Surprisingly it's the most racist bank in Northeast Ohio according to the *Plain Dealer*.

Two Cousins has weathered every store even in the face of competition in brand new buildings. Yes, there are a few new buildings, I mean younger than me anyway. One of them is full of typical hood businesses. Another has a bail bondsman and the surprisingly well-preserved remains of a full-service restaurant. It must have opened and closed when I was out of town.

Finally, I enter the shiny new welfare building that's owned by Mount Pleasant Now and no longer a welfare building. It's the home of Seeds of literacy.

Robert Vejdovec

# Changes Around East Boulevard / Martin Luther King Jr. Drive

This is a story about the changes in the area from 1962 to now. I attended Benedictine High School from 1962 to 1966 and there have been many changes since then.

There used to be a hilly field on Kinsman referred to as Kingsbury Run which is now part of Luke Easter Park. Our football team used to practice on that field area in the 60s as it was an open area where we could work out. We also practiced and played our games of baseball and tennis at the former recreation facilities on East Boulevard, now Martin Luther King Jr. Drive. This space is now a new recreation facility and also part of the park. These new recreation facilities near Kinsman are very inviting for local activities. Congratulations to the city for all their improvements.

Now the team practices on a field behind the gymnasium on school property. The new field known as Bossu Field—in honor of the former teacher and coach, Mr.

Augie Bossu—is being used for sport practices and some varsity teams other than the Benedictine varsity football team. It was once used to complete a storm shortened game because no other space was easily available.

Benedictine has also made a contribution to the area. A new chapel was built to serve the area with the old St. Benedict School and Church being closed and sold. The Abbey Chapel is a landmark to the area and serves as an anchor of faith for the community. The improvements that the monks of the Abbey have made to the School, Abbey and grounds make their campus an inviting place to visit.

The transformation over the years to the whole neighborhood makes it a pleasure to drive through. The redevelopment of housing and stores is very nice. A lot has been done in this time.

Lionel Johnson

# Reflection:
# Martin Luther King Jr. Drive

Today I write about the John Adams lunch room. My photo prompt is of John Adams in 1961. I started at Adams in 1964. My story is about my lunch room hustle. Lunches in those days cost 40 cents. It was wholesome food with the entree and usually mashed potatoes. It was always fish on Fridays for the Catholic students. My hustle was I could steal your lunch faster than it took you to stand in line. In the mornings I would ask a couple of students if they wanted my services. "I will get your lunch, the milk, napkins, everything! You just go and sit down and I will bring your tray to you"! That was my sole pitch. I would get those customers at .40 a pop! That would net me 1.20!

Eventually, I was busted and suspended for three days. When I came back to school, the assistant principal told me that I was barred from the lunch room. For the rest of my time at John Adams, I had to go home for lunch. That is my memory of the John Adams lunch room circa 1964-1967.

Rodney Pulley

# Reflection: Buckeye-Woodland

In the neighborhood of Buckeye-Woodland people was responsible. Guys and gals were more respectful to each other. Honesty is a true key, because once you step over that boundary you can't get it back. I don't like when people downgrade the Buckeye-Woodland area because it wasn't like that. It was all neighborhoods that went down in Cleveland, however due to gentrification and redlining, we lost a lot of our businesses and blacks got pushed out. This drove the value down of the neighborhood. For example, my parents' house should be worth $70,000, now it's worth $30,000 due to the environment in which it is in. Non-blacks come into our neighborhood buy up these properties, run businesses, don't have to pay taxes, and get a break.

Walking girls from school, I don't even see that anymore. It was a different era. It was a different time. Thom McCann's used to be on Buckeye. People was wearing Conley boots, now they called Chelsea boots and brothers was wearing Spatts. Spatts got the button on the side that would snap. Clothes always been an expression of your personality. Same is true for people and things that we attach to us, that is around us.

7500 Euclid Ave.    70-163 · M · 6-23-70

I see people nowadays wear the same fashion. Lets you know history repeats itself. On 131st and Kinsman it used to be Brownies pool hall. They used to shoot pool, full of hustlers. Cleveland always used to be a hustling city. You had players, pimps, hustlers. Leo's Casino was on Euclid. That's where I first saw Smokey Robinson, The Temptations, and the Supremes. All the acts used to come to Cleveland. It was a hub like Chicago or Detroit. Mostly Detroit. I just don't like to be talked about in a bad way because I seen different.

Rosemarie Fairman

# Reflection: East 93rd and Manor Ave.

I wish I could remember how old I was when Dad drove down Manor Ave. and pointed to the house he grew up in. It was dusk and just me and Dad in the car. The day was cloudy and all the houses looked the worse for wear, but the one Dad pointed to was really falling apart. There was a small gabled roof over a narrow porch. The steps looked wonky. It seemed, the other houses on the street, placed so closely together, needed to hold each other upright. We didn't do more than pause. Dad drove past a few houses to East 93rd and turned our car toward home. It was so fast, the pointed revelation, so smeared with surprise that I couldn't have told you the color of the front door.

Dad didn't talk much about his childhood. As with most quiet men, I had to listen to what dropped at odd, unexpected moments when some memory surfaced because of where we were driving, what came on TV, or what Dad might be holding in his hand. He commented, one day, that there was a factory with an open lot across from where he lived as a kid. He and his friends would play ball and get dusty-dirty before the sun started to

set and they had to go home. He implied it was the type of game where kids felt lucky if they had the right size stick because Tom or Jim didn't show up with a bat that day. The boys drew bases in the dirt and didn't dare trying to slide into home.

There were too many sharp cinders to tear knees, and they'd get whopped if they tore up their pants.

One day, we were in the kitchen peeling potatoes for dinner. I noticed Dad had stopped peeling and was looking at the spud in his hand. He told my brother and I to appreciate that we had food. He recalled one day when he was walking home and found a potato on the ground. He wanted to eat it, raw and all, but he didn't. He took it home and gave it to his grandmother who frequently cooked dinner for them. He remembered watching as Grandma Nora added the potato to the stew.

Another time, when one of us kids complained about walking home from school, he mentioned how far he had to walk to his grandparents' house after school. East 93rd was the main road that connected St. Catherine School to where his grandparents lived. He walked back-and-forth, usually with a sibling, the mile-plus from Manor Ave. where he lived with his mother, brothers, and sisters to school or to St. Catherine Church.

East 93rd is one of those long, straight Cleveland roads that slices through several neighborhoods. That first neighborhood in Dad's young life was on the side streets that ran down a few miles of East 93rd that stretched between school and supper. It is still a main north-south route that gives the driver a straight shot from Broadway to Woodhill where the road angles east. Snippets of East 93rd continue to Hough Ave., but it's not contiguous. The businesses and factories that line the wide street and fill the neighborhood where my Dad was a kid have changed. The street won't win a prize for being a pretty drive, but it's still convenient. I think of my Dad every time I drive it.

The house where Dad grew up on Manor Ave. was simply furnished. Dad's father, a cabinet maker who seemed to tower over his small wife, had built some of the chests and small tables the family used. There was also a little hutch with framed glass doors and glass knobs that his father built for his sisters to use. It held small dishes for tea parties with dolls. One evening, Dad's father came home quite sick with influenza. He went to bed and was dead the next morning. Dad was four-years-old, the second youngest of six young children.

Grandma Nora knew loss and love. She helped her daughter through the pain of burying a husband and redirecting her life. By the time my Dad was old enough to walk north on E. 93rd from St. Catherine School, it was Grandma Nora's door he opened. His mother had to go to work.

In the 30s and into the 40s, the basic modes of transportation for Dad and his family were bus, streetcar, or shoe leather. Dad's mother never learned to drive a car, but I understood that she could get anywhere she wanted in Cleveland. The quick click of her size-five pumps covered many sidewalks between bus and streetcar connections. Dad implied that he was quite

comfortable with the walk up and down East 93rd
Street from St. Catherine to his grandparents' house
or his own home. At the intersection of Manor Ave
and E. 93rd, he would pass a building that housed
apartments and a restaurant. It was a red brick estab-
lishment complete with large windows and a sign that
said "Liquor." It anchored the corner. In the 40s, the bar
was called Joe's Grill. One of Dad's frequent errands,
he recalled, was walking to that corner for a bucket of
suds. The owner came to know him well enough, so he
didn't need a note for the beer purchase. As much as he
might run or skip on the way to the corner, he had to be
very careful on the way home and not spill a drop. The
freshness of the beer was a scented memory that clung
to him.

Years later, when Dad's own granddaughter worked for
a craft brewery, she gifted him with a growler. He, with
the excitement of the boy he used to be, called his sister
over to taste and smell the memory that had stayed
with him for decades. He had never been much of a
beer drinker, but that evening he reveled in the color,
taste, and smell (most of all the memory-rich smell) of
the beer. He emphasized over and over again how care-
fully he had walked when carrying the bucket of suds.

Over the years as Grandma Nora grew small and pulled
her hair into a tight white bun, she moved in with one
of her daughters to a house on Easton Rd. It was also
off East 93rd but closer to St. Catherine Church. The
house filled with more family members, and it became
normal for the children to cook for Grandma. In the
50s when Dad, Mom, and us kids would visit Grand-
ma Nora, she'd be sitting, strategically placed in front
of the television set, in her carved platform rocker.
My siblings and I would come up to her and say hello.

She'd squint at us, reaching her hands to our arms, asking who we were. We were little shadows before her eyes, but she would brighten when Dad came over and bent his face into hers. She would breathe in his greeting and laugh. She would touch his cheek and smile a million wrinkles. The uncles would usually ask if she wanted a beer, and of course she did. Then, they would chuckle at how much she had enjoyed a previous fight she'd watched on TV, joking that she wore herself out by throwing more punches than the boxers had.

Years later, as I replayed these scenes in my head, I grew to understand how Dad grew up. By listening to the jokes the uncles and aunts would tell, I learned of the walks, the meals, and other ways Dad grew in and out of the neighborhood.

Now and then, when I would be with Dad on errands, he would comment about the various sections we drove through on Cleveland's east side. Dad worked in the flats at Republic Steel and Tubes, but he also repaired TVs in the evening. He was always searching out greasy electronics shops for just the right wires and TV tubes. He drove me though roads he just assumed I knew. If I asked a question, I'd get one back: Can't you read a map? All you have to know is that Lake Erie is north. You can find your way, can't you?

That one shadowed evening when he paused as we drove down Manor Ave. was different. It wasn't a moment for questions. His voice held a different tone, as though he had left some of his breath on the small porch, he had pointed out to me. I think I was a teen, but I may have been younger that evening. I don't know. Does one need to be a certain age to understand how you never truly leave the rooms of a house you grew up in?  And what of the streets that were walked day after day? Did his feet still know when to step off the curb or turn past Joe's Grill?

I didn't know what questions to ask when Dad pointed to the house on Manor Ave. at East 93rd. We turned north and drove further and further from the sidewalks Dad had walked so often. I remember we were quiet with each other on the drive home.

Barbara Roberson

# Third Grade

I was as very small little girl, legs as large as a Laddie pencil. Some don't know what Laddies pencils are; it was what we used in elementary school, and they were all blue.

I went to Case Woodland Elementary school on 40th and Woodland in Cleveland, Ohio. In that area was lots of older model homes, probably built in 1920 or so. Some were well kept; some were not in good shape. The point is I had to walk to school from the project tenements we lived in that was called Outhwaite Homes.

Lots of children walked this same path to Case Woodland School. Some of us were talking and laughing. Some of us walked alone. Mostly I walked with the children that lived in my circle. The walk was about 10 or 15 minutes from home. Anyway, I was not the brightest bulb in the classroom. I had a hard time comprehending most things coming from the teacher.

Math was the worst.

Apparently there had been some talk between my mother and the teacher. My mother was a stay at home mom; my dad went to work every morning at 5:30am. She was firm and stern, no jestering at all. One day, my mom was summoned to the classroom while class was going on. When she entered the room, I was petrified. All the children began to whisper, giggle and say "That's Barbara's mother."

Well, the teacher went to the board and put up a math problem. Two children were called before me, then it was my turn to go up. I don't recall the teachers name, yet she was white. That's all we were accustomed to were white teachers.

Well, as I was called I slowly went to the board, trembling in my legs ready to pee on myself. She said, "Barbara can you take the problem to the next step"? I stood there blankly, off in another world. I had no clue what to do; I had no clue what I was thinking; just numb. I could hear the children whispering and shuffling their feet under the wooden desks.

My mother and teacher were whispering to each other looking at me. I must've stood there for 15 minutes, saying nothing. My little twig legs were trembling. I just didn't know how to complete the math problem.

Eventually the teacher said have a seat. I went to my little wooden desk and sat down.

The third grade was the worst.

S. Alease Ferguson

# Coming up the Rough Side of the Mountain: Breaking the Stalemate of Discrimination

Every urban neighborhood across America has its own folk heroes and legends. I grew up in the early 1960s in Cleveland's southeast side communities of Mt. Pleasant and later Lee Harvard. Those were the years of the civil rights movement, folks moving up north to escape the domestic terrorism of southern racism and plentiful work in the auto and steel industries. It was time when hope for a better life reigned supreme. This was all before the fragmenting effects of desegregation had come about. Thus, we were still a village woven tight and strong like the finest Kinte, Adire, Oke, Bark, and Bogolanfini mud cloth. As children, we watched, learned and practiced the how to of everyday living.

My Daddy's life was a true "lift as we climb story" worth telling. In many ways, it is a vital manhood and rites of passage story all about achieving maturity through sacrifice because he loved us and our community. To be fit for duty, his meddle was tested. He made a complete revolution on his night-sea journey and a

mythic voyage across Jim Crow America, a segregated United States Army, deployment to South Korea's war theater and back home to the changing world of industrial Cleveland. In each chapter, Daddy made the choices that allowed him to play out the roles of the Warrior, Magician, the Lover, and the King. Once practiced at each, he was whole and grounded enough to lead himself and others. His daring to risk and experience life allowed him to bless the lives of others, create and inspire creativity, offer order and direction, act to protect the realm, and live with integrity.

As his eldest daughter, I had the privilege to watch the span of his career. He was a veteran Cleveland, Ohio based Black Realtor dating from the late 1950s to the eve of the new millennia. My Daddy, Louie as he was called, taught me the importance of hard work and grinding it out in order to "come up the rough side of the mountain." Louie was a crusader for black home-ownership as a dream to be achieved for both our family and his clients. He believed that homeownership was a sacred human right guaranteed under the Constitution. In his heart, it was the penultimate achievement of the American Dream. Foremost it was a demonstration of pride and self-sufficiency in service to the living and future generations.

Few recognize that housing discrimination and racial hatred are actually one and the same. Across the whole of American history, neither has ever been eradicated and likely won't be. Yet Louie was bold enough to take a deep stab at it. Throughout his career, he made a difference for his 300-customers who victoriously claimed homeownership. Since black homeownership has always been "a tough row to hoe," Louie's impact was BIG! Over and again I watched him take his clients in hand and make plain the nature of racial discrimination in America and how to overcome it. At night he studied hard to keep abreast of business ins and outs. In time, networking became his forte since you needed all sorts of friends in high places to help seal a deal. As a leader, teacher and "role model," Louie showed folks how to plan, save and mount a successful course of homeownership no matter how long it took.

In the midst of all of that success, Daddy was always modest. Though he's long gone, friends, neighbors, and customers still champion him as one "Bad-A Race Man." Yet he'd never admitted to it, while in the truest sense he was a real "freedom fighter." Anyone willing to preach, teach, and demonstrate how to of economic self-sufficiency and fuel a vision for achieving the American Dream was iconic. If you think about it, he had created a portal of the present to the future by helping folks' step through the portal of time to lay the bulwark for passing down wealth through the generations.

More than anything, I marvel at Daddy's remarkable energy and ingenuity during his years of service. He did the work with the vision and tenacity. Daddy had the drive of Hannibal of Carthage leading a legion of 30,000 soldiers, 37 elephants, and 15,000 horses across the Swiss Alps' most rugged and remote pass known as the Col Du Clapier/The Way of Hercules, charged for victory. Like the lyric from Bob Marley's rendition of "Buffalo Soldier": "...dreadlock Rasta, fighting on arrival, fighting for survival and for the soul of America," Daddy burned tons of shoe leather traveling the urban frontier. For weeks at a time, he'd canvassed whole neighborhoods block-by-block. At the same time, he was not above tromping through the seedy hallways of tenements or dingy and littered hallways of public housing estates to prospect for clients. On his walk, he spoke "truth to power" on black uplift and economic self-sufficiency. At the heart of it all, he was also the Black Panther T'Challa shouting the fierce decree of "Wakanda Forever" while "striving to create a world where black people continually triumph over the influences of imperialism, capitalism and white supremacy ." My Daddy's efforts to change the face of black homeownership in Cleveland Ohio were epic. Again, I am so grateful to have joined Daddy on his purposeful and life-changing walk.

## Louie

Louie was a handsome guy of medium height, fit and sturdy built. He was olive-tan colored with pockmarked skin and wavy coal-black hair. He had the stamina to burn and a work ethic to match. But it was his charisma that made him a natural-born salesman. By day Daddy proudly dawned his Chevrolet workman's uniform, company badge and United Auto Worker's Local 1005 membership card. Yet he poured passion into his 30-hours a week real estate gig. He earned his Broker's license in 1957 and was a card-carrying member of the National Association of Real Estate Brokers (NAREB.) for almost 40-years until his death. As a black businessman, he embodied the philosophical stances of both Booker T. Washington's works of the hand and W.E. B DuBois works of the intellect. Louie was as elegant in his workman's uniform as he was in his going to the office suit and tie, stingy brimmed hat and winged tipped shoes.

The hawk-eyed and perceptive Louie was a keen observer of people and life and would take no wooden nickels. His large beefy hands told you that he had grappled with the substance of life. At 33 he had brushed against life's thorns and brambles. He had squeaked through its openings, run up risers and skirted around blockades. Louie accepted the ambiguities and the opportunities present in a world that was neither perfect nor sane. His military deployment in Puysanyang South Korea taught him first-hand the ravages of war, sickness, starvation, and death among the refugees living in the squalid shantytowns littering the Pusan Perimeter.

Through Jim Crow, the Korean Conflict, and the Cold War, this Central High School's class of 1947 graduate journeyed full circle. Upon his return, Louie was a man on fire. He was stoked with a thirst for homeownership and his new path in real estate sales. He wanted to uplift the race and make a better world. There was no better place and time to make it, than in a city on the verge of sprawl and renowned as the "the best location in the nation." It was the place to be with its eminence as a manufacturing and cultural center and ranking as one of the nation's premier urban school districts. Cleveland's promise along with marriage and fatherhood strengthened his resolve to accomplish what they say couldn't be done and in particular what they said black people could not do. These were his bona fides. He was buoyed up by his quick wit, the will do and be better and make his girls proud. Daddy kept pushing beyond the boundaries with the certainty that there was more to life. He would work and will himself to scale the heights and seek out greener pastures beyond the Short Scovill-Bucket of Blood neighborhood of his youth.

At every turn, Louie knew what he was up against.
He was piercing the dense and poisonous layers of
racism and internalized oppression strangling blacks
and whites alike. Louie understood bigotry's soul-de-
stroying effects on the conquered masses. He saw it's
disabling effects on upward social mobility and inter-
generational progress. Deep down inside he felt the
pangs of every African American's longing for a home
place. Louie said that our thirst for a home place was
lodged in our DNA. He said that these cell memories
went back to our memories of capture and binding by
chains, ropes, nets, and wooden yokes; the horrific Mid-
dle Passage, years under the lash and the long walk to
freedom from the plantations to the unknowns of city
life during the Reconstruction. In his view "having a
home of one's own would always be a powerful lure for
all African Americans." He was absolutely vehement
that homeownership was a powerful act of "resistance."
Engaging in the struggle to strike down the barriers of
race and place was "that glorious grab of the brass ring
and the self-defined seizure of equal access."

According to Louie, there were all kinds of social and
historical factoids, concerning housing discrimination
against Blacks. It was all mired in racial subordination
and chattel slavery in the U.S. He described racism
as a sullied part of the American heritage. He said it
was like a festering wound that could not be healed
or debrided even across the epochs of slavery, Recon-
struction and Jim Crow and the desegregated society.
Housing discrimination took the form of denied access;
redlining and blockbusting, invalidation of deeds; tax
penalties, and predatory lending girded in sub-prime
loans. He said that the "politicians, urban planner, and

banks were all to blame." They'd made policies for the denial of mortgage loans based on a homebuyer's race or a neighborhood's racial mix. At the same time, it was allowable for White communities to buck and stonewall by passing new zoning and land-use restrictions that expressly kept Black people out. I remember the short-lived hope that came from the passage of the federal Fair Housing and Mortgage Disclosure Act 1968. It turned out to be just another gimmick and a broken promise with numbers that did not bear out. It was 40 acres and a mule all over again and the status quo remained. How could there ever be a change when European Americans have always been ten times wealthier than African Americans and occupy 64 percent homeownership.

In the years after the passage of the Fair Housing and Mortgage Disclosure Act of 1968 Black homeownership rates kept sliding down year after year to a pitiable 41.2. Yet before the Civil Rights movement 50% of "Coloreds" or "Negroes" as we were called, owned homes. Daddy used to say that it was only half the story when researchers blamed the declines on the "lack of affordable housing and stricter lending for first-time buyers." He said the real truth was, that discrimination on the educational and employment fronts short-circuited our abilities to prosper.

I honor Louie's struggle and ethic of hard work and the will to bring the legions along for the cause of homeownership. His clientele were beleaguered so he had to reinvigorate a sense of racial pride and self-agency. He worked hard to replace the maiming Oppressor induced mindsets of self-hatred and inequality. It meant imploding such divisive myths as: "Black folks live poor in substandard housing and squalid conditions only because they want to," or "Only uppity Negroes of the Bourgeoisie could buy homes." To get into the homeownership game he helped his customers cast aside fears and stereotypes, resolve, dream, locate sideline hustles, and save money. It took that kind of action to turn the tables on housing discrimination.

These were still times of unchecked violence, and white supremacist skull and crossbones tactics aimed at keeping us out. He also prayed that one day that America's real and fictional Pleasantville's, and all that "Not in My Backyard" (NIMBY), and "oops here they come and there goes the neighborhood" business would all go the way of the dinosaur. He'd tell clients that the times were a-changing and to press full steam ahead without blinking. The threats of "N__ Stay in your place" scare tactics: harassment, Molotov cocktail lobbed, and gangland-style car bombings were real. We had to author our own rights; summon enough courage to go forward. He soldiered on with the mantra of "all we can do is act on our own behalf and find every way possible to crawl up from the bottom to break the stalemate and equalize the power."

*Passing on the Trade*

Louie was born into an entrepreneurial family and so he believed in the old adage that "the cobbler's children should never be without shoes." It was custom that we learned the family business. Our training in the Real Estate started early at home and in the field. It was welded into our family's lifestyle and cultural and linguistic framework. By the time I was in kindergarten, I knew the meaning of such terms as agent, broker, client, closing costs, commission, deeds, lender, mortgages, loan, inspection, points, and titles. As the proud family receptionist, I parroted my message taking using the script of: "Hello this is the Louis residence, may I help you? May I please take your name and telephone number? And Mr. Louie will call you back promptly." By the time I was in the first grade, I could tell you the stepwise process of a home sale. By third grade, Daddy taught me how to calculate the monthly charges and interest rates on fifteen, twenty and thirty-year mortgages.


At least twice a month Sissy and I got the chance to see the city and help Daddy prospect for new buyers and sellers. It was the whole enchilada of "dressing for success," business deportment and lessons on Cleveland history, geography, and home architecture. On the ride we'd take turns standing behind Daddy, hugging his neck as he tooled around the city in our old blue and crème Studebaker with the rusted-out bumper. Through the Studebaker's concave windshield, Sissy and I glimpsed the wide world of Cleveland, Ohio. Up from the core rose the east side's black neighborhoods of Outhwaite, Garden Valley, Kinsman, Hough and Cedar-Central, and Glenville. They all fanned out from the center city like the spokes of a bicycle wheel cut in half. I say half because we never traveled to the west side. Daddy said that we'd only go where he could capture a market of buyers and sellers. While prospecting we learned that each street was its own delight. Whether you were on a street, a drive, an alley, a court or a place, there was always a mixture of Cape Cods, Century homes, California and Mid-century Bungalows, Duplexes, Prairie Styles, and Long Porch houses. Sometimes you'd only see four, eight and twelve suite apartment buildings with a Victorian Painted Lady or two. In time we learned more about architectural design, a home's "bones," curb appeal, the pitch of a roof, best-selling colors, landscaping and all the flourishes that clinch a sale.

*Securing Wealth for Future Generations*

Then something wonderful happened!

April 16, 1961 is a day forever etched in memory. That's when my parents became first-time homeowners. They had worked hard and sacrificed much. For months Daddy had promised that we'd soon move from Aunt Annie and Uncle Drew's second-floor apartment to a home of our own. He said that it would be a big house with a sprawling backyard. It turned out that we moved a one street north and two blocks down into Cleveland's second Gold Coast, in the Lee Harvard Neighborhood. It was the area's last street of majesty, filled with large circa 1922 homes built strong like Sherman tanks. The grandeur of these homes was matched only by the swaths of century-old Dutch Elms, Red Maples, Oaks, Sycamores and Pines. Each home was a distinct, well-kept, and welcoming vignette of architectural design. Some had long porches, others had cropped porches with canvass awnings, and some had stoops. In late spring the lawns were manicured, and the pussy willows and forsythia were in bloom. Soon there would be pops of color from azaleas, and rhododendrons, hydrangea, holly and boxwood shrubs. Our backyard was incredible! Stepping out of the car Sissy and I started the wild imaginings of our yard in summer. There were grand possibilities of family and friends gathering at umbrella tables, and Mommy grilling ribs and franks over the brick oven pit. Off to the side, we'd place our badminton net and further back our croquette court. Most beauteous was the mature grape arbor buttressed by a weathered wooden pergola that beckoned "Welcome friend! Come sit and rest."

Then Daddy opened the doors to a wonderland. At first, Sissy and I stared awe-struck. It was move-in ready with open spaces and nooks and crannies galore. We could not resist sliding across the hardwood floors that shone like glass. We chortled with laughter at the reverb of our voices echoing in the emptiness. We couldn't stop opening and shutting the palatial French doors that separated the salon from the formal dining room. During the grand tour we imagined ourselves, living, eating, sleeping and playing in its every square inch. We had a cook's kitchen and a breakfast nook. Upstairs we had three bedrooms and two baths. Our basement had a finished rec-room with a bar paneled in knotty pine, and a washroom the length of the house. Our long-enclosed sun porch brought an added sense of fun and a chance to look about the treetops and the houses as far as three streets over.

As we played Mommy and Auntie triumphantly marched from room to room singing spirituals and anthems of deliverance acapella. Together they sang fervently like gospel greats Clara Ward and Mahalia Jackson. They christened the house with their exuberance and tears of joy. For hours they sang an old-time medley of Gospel songs like "Blessed Assurance":

> *Jesus is mine, oh what a foretaste of glory divine.*
> *Oh, what a foretaste of glory divine!*
> *Heir of salvation, purchase of God,*
> *Born of His Spirit, washed in His blood.*

Refrain:

*This is my story, this is my song,*
*Praising my Savior all the day long;*
*This is my story, this is my song,*
*Praising my Savior all the day long.*

Perfect submission, perfect delight, and my favorite,
"How Great Thou Art":

*O Lord my God, when I am in awesome wonder,*
*consider all the worlds*
*Thy Hands have made; I see the stars, I hear the*
*rolling thunder,*
*Thy power throughout the universe displayed.*

Then they ended with a rousing chorus of "How I Got
Over," my soul looks back and wonders how I got over?

On that day of jubilation, we had miraculously crossed
the Jordan. My Daddy's demonstration of homeown-
ership was no small feat for a black family then, or
now. As night fell, he and Mommy sat on the foot of the
stairs. He wrapped his arms around her and exclaimed
"Baby we did it! Now I am the real McCoy. I am a re-
al-life role model for my clients. You know that most
people think that the real estate business is all book
knowledge and formulas. But now I have walked the
paces and joined the club."

*Breaking the Barrier*

There is something suspense filled about moving into a
neighborhood on the brink of transition. To the good,

we had terra firma and new-found status in Lee Harvard. After all, we had landed in Cleveland's "suburb in the city" and "the New Gold Coast" bordering on the suburbs of Shaker, Warrensville, and Garfield Heights. Yet, we still lived in the shadow of violence and discord. Years before there had been the infamous 1953 "Paint Bombing" of Wendell and Genevieve Stewart's home on Talford Avenue. Though they were courageous and toughed it out, it took almost seven years before the steady influx of other black families. At once we saw the rapid disbanding of an Italian and Eastern European Catholic enclave, and the ramp-up of a high flying black middle-class skyrocketing towards success. Most of our black neighbors had migrated to Cleveland, code named as "Station Hope" to flee the domestic terrorism and poverty of the South. These dignified two-parent headed working households enjoyed the post-World War II boom of modernity, good jobs, and gracious living. They were professionals and skilled trade's people who'd graduated from Cheney State, Hampton, Howard, North Carolina A&T, Tennessee State, West Virginia State, Voorhees, and Wilberforce. Here up north, they had per capita earnings that exceeded many a white suburban household. Because of it, we came to be known as "Uppity Negroes." As a house proud and determined lot, our parents would brook no intimidation or racial animus.

In the closing days of the white flight era, we gained a brief but easy rapport with our neighbors. They were the Schuler's, Feig's, Reba's, Rini's, Fazio's, Pilch's, and the Geronimo's. The snide politics of race and place dictated their southward and westward expansions. Off into the wilds, they went like doves released from a magician's box. They filled the new bedroom communities of Bedford, Brecksville, Parma and Middleburg Heights, Solon, and Strongsville. Every "Sold" sticker pasted over a "For Sale" sign heralded imminent departure, and a peaceful concession to change that only promoted more of the same.

Coming up the rough side of the mountain, Daddy showed me and Sissy that one job is never enough. According to Daddy only thrift, money made honest and piecemeal, stored rolled-up in a giant pickled pigs feet jar, and seasoned with prayer, meditation, vision and elbow grease will turn the wheel that spins the gold. He instilled in us that only diligence, gratitude, persistence, and steadfast action leads to the manifestations of dreams. Because of it, he kept the promise that the closeness of our small apartment was but a gateway to the future. And there was more, as the saga continued.

# Part II: What We Need

Jamie Hinton

# Now I Know Who I Am

I've been running for so long
Never had nothing, not even a home
I played the games you wanted me to play
I thought to myself this is not the way
Who am I?
Listening to you, I may not see another day
I'm living through you that's why
I'm not sure who I am
I'm so tired of all this drama

So I woke up and took a look around
and guess what I found?
I found me.
Oh my God what a relief!
I look in the mirror and I saw for the first time
A smart person
A beautiful person
Someone I never knew
Lord have mercy!
It's me, hello me, nice to meet you
I am worthy of anything
I can do anything

I have God on my side
Thank you God for helping me find out
Who I am
I'm smart
I'm a child of God
That's who I am
And I'm happy to meet me again!

Willie Naps

# The Height

The fam was all packed in my little rust colored Corolla.
Penny was beside me, riding shotgun. Penny's moth-
er—but I called her Ma because she was more mother
to me than my own—was in the back, behind Penny.
The girls were sprawled out beside Ma on the fold-
down section that connected the hatchback rear with
the backseat area. We were in the drive-in on Miles, the
smell of butter in the air.

Eddie Murphy and Arsenio Hall were cracking up the
crowd in *Coming to America*. We heard the dude next
to us tell his carload, "Man, I used to chase that nigga
home from school every day!" Then he fell silent as he
contemplated the lost opportunity this recollection
implied. He could be in Eddie's entourage right now;
instead, he was paying to watch the kid he'd bullied on
the big screen, Arsenio.

There we were, a late 20th Century American family,
three generations of mixed culture, well, maybe one
culture that I'd crossed into. This was the best it gets.
I had a loving family, finally and I got to provide for all.

That's my American Dream, and now, my history. My romances had moved on, but these ladies are still the core of my fam. Rest in peace Ma. All Love.

Oluremi Ann Oliver
# Becoming an Elder

Becoming an elder has afforded me time. Not because there is suddenly more time. Not because time has slowed magically for me. No, neither is true. What has occurred to me is that my relationship to time, my thinking about time, has changed. I no longer speed through anticipating the time, or the next time, or even the last time. Now, I have been afforded the time to reflect. I have been afforded the time to look back and to see with 'new' eyes what is happening now.

My favorite place to do this is at my dining room table that sits directly in front of a large picture window. The view from that window is an empty lot, meaning no house stands there. It is an open field that I can view through the Catalpa and Mulberry trees that line my fence separating my property from the next. What I see is a daily reminder of life and change. The birds that rotate through the field and trees from sun up to sun down.

Naima Omar

# Not Me

*The heart is more treacherous than anything and is desperate. – Jeremiah 17:9*

He wasn't cute but he looked like a hardworking man with his silver truck and overalls.

His introduction wasn't original, but it wasn't disrespectful either.

"No sir I don't need a ride. I'm just going to the library up the street." She wasn't really going anywhere she was just looking at butterflies.

"You should go to the Shaker library. Its better. I'm going in that direction. Let me take you. A beautiful young lady like you shouldn't be walking in all this heat."

She thought to herself, well, you only live once and got in the truck. Maybe this guy could be one of the men she was always hearing about that bought nice things

for young women. Maybe they could fall in love and get married. She wouldn't know unless she tried.

During the short ride to the suburban library he asked her what she liked to do for fun.

She said she wrote poetry. It wasn't true, it just seemed like a cool thing to say.

It wasn't hard to embellish. She told him her favorite poet was Maya Angelou. And she liked to write about nature. As she heard herself saying the words it sounded like a really good idea.

He said he was going to the library for a computer class when he was done, and that he would take her back home.

Completely plausible.

She didn't make it to whatever section contained Maya Angelou. Instead she picked up a novel about an African girl named Binti who had a space alien for a best friend. The story was so different from anything she had ever read she almost felt as if books like this had previously been illegal. After about an hour the man with the silver truck came back to see if she was ready to go back home. She owed too many library fines to check the book out. She wanted to stay but she was ashamed to tell him.

When they got back in the truck, he told her he needed to go back to his house to pick up some tools before he went on his next job. He told her about his business and all the problems he had with dishonest employees and deadbeat clients. There was nothing overtly unbelievable about anything he said. His house was only a few blocks from the library.

He invited her in and offered her a drink. She went in the house. The layout was like that of her aunt's house.

He was very talkative. He must have thought she was planning on opening a construction business and needed to hear every little detail. She tried her best to listen and be polite.

"Why aren't you drinking?"

She didn't want the drink

"One drink won't hurt you sweetheart. I'm a good man. I just want you to relax and have a good time. I could be a good man for a girl like you."

She had a few smart friends. One of her friends had told her something very valuable a while back.

People who say "I'm a good man" are very seldom good men.

"I'm ready to go home," she said.

"Relax a minute enjoy a drink with me I'll take you home later."

"You don't have to drive me. I can walk its not that far. It was nice meeting you."

"Bitch, you ain't going nowhere!" He spoke with misplaced confidence. She left the house. He didn't follow her. She wasn't sure if he would come after her later. What only 20 minutes ago had looked like a lovely suburb suddenly resembled a ghost town. She traveled a few blocks and said a quick prayer. Soon she saw a rusty Mazda containing someone's harried mama.

As the mom pulled up to the stop sign the escapee flagged her down and implored. "Can I please use your phone? I have to get away from over here. "

"What wrong sweetie?"

"You see that truck up there? I was in that house and I could barely get out. This man was trying to keep me there."

"So, you need to go in the opposite direction."

"Yes Please."

"Get in. Where are you trying to go? "

"143rd."

When the Mom inhaled again, she could smell the girl's fear. She unlocked her phone. "You should call somebody."

The girl didn't take the phone.

"Sweetie if a man wants to talk to you, he can talk to you on the phone. If he really likes you, He won't rush you."

The girl sighed, "I know, I know, believe me I won't be doing this again."

It had been years since the older woman had been on 143rd.

There was a lot more garbage than she remembered.

The girl's aunt was on the porch.

The harried mom doubled back to Walgreens so she could use the ATM and get her rent money together.

D.L. Ware

# Conversations and the Journey;
# Blue Line Transit

For the moment
let us contemplate
the past
our paths
desires
our will to survive
and as we share
this space and time

know that
it is guaranteed
we all have

struggles.

Louis McCoy

# A Vacation

Although I enjoyed the Carnival Cruise Line
Eighty-five thousand drowned
First visit was to Sotheby's. There I met men, women,
and children
I met the well-dressed wealthy and rich, mixed with the
scantily clad
Outside I bought beautiful jade and turquoise trinkets
and artifacts, from the few survivors of chicken pocks
and diphtheria
I hid from the ward between the brothers
Some brothers instituted feudalism for farming
I visited their farms
The fields were snowy white with abundant crops as
far as one could see
Some grew big yellow and brown fruit that dangle high
in the trees.
I knew how many marbles were in the jar, but not the
name of all state judges
How could I? I had not read in three hundred and fifty
years.
The downtowns were full of white faces with suits and
ties
I've seen enough
I should get back on my ship

Danielle N. Dixon

# We are not these ruins

Will they find our pride amongst broken clay pots bur-
ied beneath the soil?
Will they know we were not just civilized, but cultured?
Will they know we turned the remnants of white flight
into the pride of the black family?

Will they know we are not these ruins?

Will they know we came from slavery, through Jim
Crow
By way of Alabama
By way of Milledgeville, Georgia
By way of short Scovill
And landed on this small plot of promised land where
Kinsman and Union meet?

Will they see our hand in the shaping of America and
be proud?
Or, will they tell our stories as failure, represented by
boarded up houses and empty lots?

Will they know we are not these ruins?

Will they know that before the windows got broken
and the siding was stripped this house was our ances-
tors' dream?
Will they know that before the overgrown bushes we
had impeccably manicured lawns?
Will they know we were an entire street of black home-
owners just two generations past slavery?

Will they know we are not these ruins?

Will they know were not Moynihan statistics?
      We were two-parent households
      We were marriages that lasted longer than 30
      years
      We were business owners in our communities

Will they know we were the sacrifice so that our
children could forge their destinies beyond the red
lines? Will they know our legacy was not subdued by
this decaying infrastructure, but transcended it?
Will they see the grassy lots left behind as blank canvas
for descendants to start something new?

Will they know we are not these ruins?

# Part III: What We Love

Bernice Watson

# Thank You Mama (You Are Appreciated)

Good morning everyone
Happy Mother's Day
To all the mothers that are here today
This message is for
All the mothers around the world
Especially mine
Who I lost in 2006 to colon cancer
Thank you, mama, for
Carrying me in your belly for nine months
Thank you for not aborting me
Thank you for loving and caring for me
And protecting me from harm
Thank you for teaching me my ABC's and 123's
And teaching me to ride my bike
With the training wheels attached
Thank you for packing my lunch for school
And teaching me to
Read and write
Thank you for teaching
Me how to tie my shoestrings
And teaching me how to tell time
Thank you, Big Mama

For the manners you taught that I use today
But I am so sorry, Big Mama
That I was not the best granddaughter
Evil in all my ways
But you moved me anyway
Thank you for shelter
A bed to lay my head
You didn't have to do it
But you did
Rest in people grandmother
I love you

I also remember as a child, mama
When you would treat me
To Wendy's downtown
And Woolworths
Where I got my first ear piercing
And how you would come pick me up
From school
And we would go to the movies
I miss those times
But you are resting in God's peace now
May I see you in Heaven one day
What a wonderful mother
You were to us, me and my brothers
Even though you never said it
You showed us love

Thank you so much, Big Mama and mama
I know you are smiling down
Thank you, Lord, for all mothers
Around the world
That are single or married
Thank you for being the backbone of the family
Being a wife, mother, sister, auntie, and friend
Thank you

Thank you, Lord, for Renee for cooking
For the Winton Manor on Tuesdays
Lord I thank you for Natalie's kind words
Of wisdom and encouragement

Lord, thank you for Virginia
For teaching us women about the Bible
At Sunday's Bible study
And for all the mothers I didn't name
May God bless you
In all ways
Once again, thank you mothers
Around the world

Thank you, thank you
Thank you
And I love you

Your sista in Christ,
Bernice

Rose M. Griffin

# The Family

Mama's in the kitchen cooking good food,
Daddy's in the garage under the hood,
Chris is upstairs ironing some clothes,
Rees is in the basement, washing by the loads,
Nita's upstairs making the beds,
I'm in the bathroom, washing my head,
Michael's outside digging a hole,
The twins are somewhere playing the role,
And that's my family as my story is told.

Lionel Johnson

# Friend

During my formative years, Carl McManus was one of my best friends.  This is his story.

Carl and I met in 1959 during the summer before fifth grade.  That summer our family had just moved from Garden Valley to 3461 East 117th street, seven houses from Union Avenue.  Mount Pleasant Elementary School, with its playground teeming with kids, was right across from our house.  The first time I saw Carl he was looking like Spanky of the Little Rascals, wearing a whirly bird hat and striped tee- shirt.  He was chubby and cherubic.  Jocular like Spanky he was doing something funny in the playground.  I am amazed by the boy.  Being new to the neighborhood I ask the other children,

"Who is that?"

"That's Carl."

We became close through the years with never a cross

word between us. Carl and I played and walked and talked in the Mount Pleasant area in scruffy jeans and tennis shoes. Like the time we went to Miss Sally's house. He asked me, "Do you want to go over to Miss Sally's house wit' me? She will give us some milk and cookies."

Of course, I said yes. Carl's mother died two years before I met him. Miss Sally is a friend and mother figure to Carl's family who lives on 142nd street near Bartlett.

Imagine a Mount Pleasant free of trash on the sidewalks, or garbage in the streets. Every house, every apartment building is well maintained. There were peach and cherry trees and grape vines in the backyards. Crab apple and plum trees grew on vacant lots. The fruit trees gave their fragrance to the area. It was surely a pleasant place to live.

We left the playground going up Union to 131st. As we went down 131st, we passed Mayfair Dry Cleaners, and Charles Dickens Elementary, and the Pet Shop with puppies in the window at the corner of Benham Avenue. Then the Fourth District Police Station. We came to shady Bartlett and go up to 142nd.

We got to Miss Sally's house and sure enough she set out a plate of cookies for us and two glasses of milk. This was heaven for a ten-year-old boy. We ate the snack, thanked Miss Sally and retraced our steps with Carl keeping me laughing the whole way back. We heard a sonic boom just before we get to the playground on a perfect summer day.

Then there was the time we went to Geauga Lake Amusement Park. Carl's father worked at Thompson Products which later became TRW. They had the company picnic there.

Carl and I rode the roller coaster 27 times. That was the day I first tasted custard. Carl was a newspaper boy for the afternoon newspaper, the now defunct Cleveland Press. On collection day, I would go with him. After he put money aside for the newspaper man, he would buy candy, pop, potato chips, and Hostess Twinkies for us.

A few years later we were in Nathan Hale Junior High on East Boulevard. This was the time of the civil rights movement. The civil rights organizers had planned an event called Freedom Day, a boycott of the Cleveland Public Schools. On the appointed day you were not to go to school, but to report to your neighborhood church. Our church was Second Tabernacle Baptist Church on 119th and Union. There, adults would monitor us and be our teachers for the day. Like in Sunday school. Dick Gregory, the famous comedian and activist was to go around to all the Churches and speak to groups of people.

Carl wasn't at the church at first, but by the time Dick Gregory showed up, Carl was there. Dick Gregory spoke and then he split. He had a lot of churches to go to on Freedom Day.

Somebody asked Carl where he had been. Carl said that he went to school. A white person asked him, what was he doing there? Someone at the church asked the same thing. Carl said he just wanted to see. He said there were no black students there, so he left and came to the church.

Carl is light-skinned and by the time that we were in John Adams High School on 116th and Corlett they start calling him White Man. Some called him Hunky behind his back. As we become older, Carl took it upon himself to school me on the ways of the world. We are no longer boys in jeans and Spanky hats, but urbane young men in the latest styles wearing cologne and alligator shoes. He would say, "Shorty, it's like this..." and the Dude would be right.

He said world events often came down to economics. Big money rules the world. For example, Africans sold millions of us to the Europeans for gold and silver. Carl told me things that people on the news would say later.

We went to school sharp every day, but on Friday's we were extra sharp. On Thursday evenings we got together at Carl's crib on 116th street and watched color TV while we got our outfits together. We were not sharp by accident. We worked at it. We went over our clothing with a fine-tooth comb, cutting away loose threads with a small pair of scissors. We shined our shoes. I can't tie a knot in a necktie so Carl would tie mine for me, a Windsor or some other fancy knot. We talked about what colors went with what. For example, no brown shoes with grey pants. If we wore a sport coat and a pair of pants, the coat was always darker than the pants. We never put stripes and plaids or checks together. When I saw people do that it hurt my eyes.

On Fridays we always wore a suit and tie. We came up with creative ways to wear the classic black suit. Carl started wearing his black suit with a blue shirt instead of the traditional white. I began wearing my black suit with an iridescent orange shirt and black tie. If we wore a hat, the hat must match the color of the shoes.

After our Thursday night prep, Carl and I would step in John Adams at eight thirty on Friday as clean as the board of health. You might have thought we were some hip young teachers or something, though no teacher was as clean as us. Going to school dressed up made it exciting for me. Exhilarating, if you will. The weekend started on Fridays. The parties, the football games. I would say to myself, "Somebody's daughter is going to like me tonight." I was dressed like I stepped out of the pages of GQ. We often looked at *Gentlemen's Quarterly Magazine* for tips on how to dress well.

We knew that we had a better chance with the girls if we were dressed to the nines and had a little money in our pockets to buy her a banana boat at Vince's ice cream stand on 116th and Kinsman, or to take her to see the Temptations at Leo's Casino or the Music Box on Euclid Avenue. Girls, girls, girls. The young ladies were sharp too with fabulous dresses and skirts, pretty shoes and fine hairdos.

Carl did not carry books at school. There was this group of four beautiful girls who were all sisters and cousins. We called the girls the Four Tops. They carried Carl's books. Picture Carl walking the halls of John Adams looking like a playboy on the French Riviera with the Four Tops trailing carrying their books and his.

We would play football at Woodhill Park. We went there to play one Saturday, but no one else showed up. We were 16 years old at this time. Carl said that we should bury the football equipment in the bushes and go downtown and look for jobs. So, we did that. I always took that to mean that it was time to grow up and stop playing boy's games.

We did not find jobs that day but we did later. A lot of us had after school jobs then. Our parents could not afford to buy the expensive dress clothing that we were wearing by this time. It was cool. If our parents gave us room and board we would work to buy our own reptile skin shoes, Italian knit shirts, sansabelt pants and cashmere overcoats.

Carl got me a dishwashing job at a new restaurant at the intersection of Richmond and Chagrin roads. I would catch the 14 Kinsman to the end of the line at 159th street. Then I would catch the #5 Chagrin. Carl told me, "The Chagrin bus is port of call. There ain't no bus stops up on Chagrin. You tell the bus driver where you want to get off."

That part of Chagrin Boulevard was not developed then. There were trees and green areas on both sides of the road. I used the money I made at the restaurant to buy more clothes. He was always helping me out. When we would go downtown to buy clothes, Carl would buy his stuff and I would buy mine. Then he would buy me a sport coat, or a pair of pants. He saved his money, so he always had more than I did. Like they say on the corner, "I raised that boy." He did in many ways.

When we were 17 it was a very good year. Carl, Lil' Mike, Tall Andy and I would go up to the state liquor store on 140th and Kinsman. It was across from the A&P Super Market, Society National Bank and the Mount Pleasant Library. We would wait outside for a kindly looking person and ask if they would buy us a pint of Ten High Bourbon. Completing that part of our mission, we walked down busy Kinsman Road and hung around a corner store and asked someone to buy a quart of Stroh's beer, a local brew, for us.

Then one of us went in the store and bought a 16-ounce bottle of RC Cola to mix with the cheap bourbon. We got all of that for under three dollars. Cool, now we went to Lil' Mike's basement on 118th around the corner from the poolroom and the four of us would get rip roaring drunk.

Carl had a great attitude about life. Where I was full of teenage angst, the vagaries of life did not bother Carl. I never saw him in a cross mood. If something bad happened to him or if he suffered some kind of personal loss he would say, "You cain't cry over spilt milk." His mind was clear free of any rancor or bitterness. I didn't understand positive and negative energy then, but Carl was all positive.

We graduated from John Adams in June 1967. The Hippies and counterculture people called the summer of '67 the Summer of Love. For blacks it was another long hot summer of strife. Urban riots broke out again. The most well-known being the riot in Newark, New Jersey. Yet when I look back, it was the summer of love for us too. Mount Pleasant was still in its prime and we were young. We enjoyed that summer more than any other.

Towards the end of the summer of love, Carl told us that he was leaving Cleveland to live with relatives in South Carolina. On the Saturday evening before Carl's departure our group of friends copped some reefer and got together in Lil' Mike's basement to reminisce about good times. Then we hung out on Kinsman Road and watched all of the action on the avenue. You could have fun just by being on the corner.

After a while Lil' Mike and Tall Andy split to the crib. Carl and I were standing on the corner of 116th and Kinsman in front of Lee's Dry Cleaners. Kinsman was still buzzing with activity with cars going by and young lovers out for the evening.

I asked Carl, "When are you comin' back?"

He told me, "I ain't neva' comin' back."

"You ain't? On the serious side?"

He shook his head, no.

I was stunned by Carl's statement, but I told him I would be at his crib in the morning to see him off. By this time we had moved from 117th to 133rd near Lambert.

In the morning I put on a blue suit with matching lizard skin slip on shoes and slid down to Carl's pad to say goodbye. I knocked on the door of their neat brick two-family crib. His sister Barbara, a pretty fair skinned girl with long straight hair, opened the door and told me, "Carl is gone."

Damn, I missed him. I wanted to see my friend off. I shambled back to the pad kind of down-hearted.

I never saw Carl again.

*Postscript*

Over the decades I wondered why Carl never came back to Cleveland. He had family here. And friends. He never had a fight with anyone the whole time I knew him. I just couldn't understand it. Once I told my girlfriend about him and our friendship since we were little boys.

I was going with Paulette then and she told me, "He probably thinks about you too sometimes."

I heard that Carl joined the Marine Corps. Someone that we knew saw Carl in Hawaii. He was recovering from wounds suffered fighting in Viet Nam. Carl stayed in the Corps after the war, serving with honor and attaining the rank of Sergeant.

Then in the seventies I heard he was in the Philippine Islands and married to a Filipino woman. I was thinking well, Carl is light- skinned and he would fit in well with the people over there. Then I heard that he was living in the western United States. But he never came east to Cleveland. One time in the late nineties, Tall Andy said, "We oughta' get ourselves together one day and go find White Man." I don't think White Man wanted to be found.

Just last year in 2018 I attended a picnic that Barbara and Carl's brother James McManus host every June at Woodhill Park. They call it the Mount Pleasant Old School Picnic.

All of us baby boomers who lived in Mount Pleasant and went to John Adams High show up.

James is the oldest of the siblings. They call him, "Mac", or "Butch." I never knew him to have a fight either. Mac is a tough Dude. No one ever dared to mess with him or insult him in any way. They have a baby sister named Marylyn who has gone to live with the lord. I'm talking to Barbara as smoke from the grill drifts in my face. I'm still confused why Carl never came back to Cleveland and shaking my head I say, "I don't know why Carl never came back, I..."

Barbara cuts me off saying, "Carl lived as a white man." I raise my head. Now it all makes sense. My friend left here to join the white world. That's why he told me he was never coming back. He didn't want to travel back and forth between both worlds. I always thought Carl would stay here and struggle with us since he knew everything. And he did. But why should he stay here and struggle with us when he could go someplace where no one knows him and be white and enjoy all the opportunities that go with that. Carl's decision to live white comes as a complete surprise to me. He never said anything disparaging about being black. He was of the people.

That fall we elected Carl Stokes as Mayor. The black pride movement was going strong. Things were looking up for black people. Barbara pulled out her phone and showed me a picture of Carl wearing a suit. Carl was a full-sized man. He always did look good in a suit. If I didn't know, would I think he was white? Yes, I would. His wife didn't know. Barbara told me that Carl's wife put white on his death certificate. She didn't know he was born black. I look at the photo again. There are no lines in Carl's face, no signs of distress. He made the right decision for him.

Barbara tells me of Carl's numerous professional accomplishments as a white man. I smile. My friend took advantage of the opportunities that he received. I understand Carl's decision to live white. He found success. We all want to succeed. I stumbled through life on rutted roads. I selfishly maintain that my life would have been better had Carl stayed in Cleveland. He would have guided me, steered me to the right track. He would have told me about a good job. We were close, but not like brothers. You have to have a brother; it's forced on you by nature. On the other hand, sincere friendship is driven by common needs and shared philosophies, especially if one of the friends is always telling jokes.

I don't begrudge my friend for his decision to live white. As they sing in the old Negro Spiritual, "I will see you bye and bye."

I will see him again. I'll say, "Let's go over to Miss Sally's for milk and cookies." Or, "Man, let's go downtown and buy some clothes."

Rest easy my friend I will see you bye and bye.

Kisha Nicole Foster

# Wired Image

telephone poles are cemeteries
vigil place holders of people
shot
stabbed
taken by violence
wails covering curb
place holders of
balloons
posters
pictures
a disarray of community
put on pause
sadness hits me as I ride
past inner city gravesites
broken cries stifled
place holders of
tears
wails
salt is the taste that stains my lips
jagged language is muted
nose clogged
broken people fixing telephone poles
with no parking signs
there's dying allowed here tho

there is a diminishing of a people here
our babies don't cry
anymore for help
they cuss and twerk
with decorative balloons
mothers with swollen eyes
more swollen bellies
fathers with guns in small of back
more ammo in the pistol than brains
they crowd around saying
"Damn nigga, not you"
say
"Damn my G, what happened"
internalizing pain
don't know grief, so can't call healing
don't know it's a systemic death trap
so can't find a way out
all's we know
are details:

a car was chasing my friend
down Wade Park at high speed
in the wee hours of mourning
she tried to make a
left turn on 63rd
her car hydroplaned
hit the curb
flew over the field
through the tree branches
crashed into the second floor
of the house
behind the field
went through a bedroom and bathroom
the engine was left in the house
the car landed in the driveway
she died
her dog lived.

Stuart M. Terman

# WHERE YOU BE GOIN..? 1956

*'patois: (pat' wa') n*

*'a regional dialect: ... substandard speech, the special
jargon of a group'*

*Ref: the American Heritage Dictionary,
second ed. Pg. 910*

The speech of the neighbors of my grandparents, with
whom I lived as child off Kinsman, was as familiar as
the Yiddish that they spoke to me with one such gentle
speaker helping a boy find his way home.


The Cleveland Museum of Art was offering free classes
that spring, and Mother signed me up before the muse-
um officials changed their minds, and we arrived that
Saturday for my initial painting class.


After the lesson Mother showed me how to leave the
building, go to East Blvd, and walk to the Cedar Rapid
where she said that I'd "need to get on the 32-B bus,"

one of many that converged at that station, to get home.

She actually just explained and pointed but thought it redundant to walk me there. My nodding indicated to her that I understood, and my nodding to me indicated bewilderment at this complicated plan. She was pointing to a location beyond the horizon, and at that time I was quite short.

Saturday—the next lesson—I was dropped off, told to "have a nice morning," and the used Buick drove away, carrying her off to work.

At noon the class was dismissed and I went out the museum's front doors past the Thinker statue and walked towards the noise of Euclid Ave. to where Severance Hall welcomes concert goers. Traffic raced in two directions, four if you count East Blvd., with Adelbert Road adding more cars, although I didn't know this street's name at the time. It was simply adding to the confusion.

I looked lost because I was lost, and stood for three or four light changes. A downtown #6 bus briefly stopped, expecting me to get on. The mailbox and the street marker looked quietly back at me, and the large elm tree across the street, now long gone, also of no help.

Lots of white people—students whom I would join 10 years later—contributed to the people at that intersection. There were very few black people except for one older, tired-appearing lady in a thin coat, crossing towards me while carrying a large, heavy shopping bag.

As she crossed the street she looked up, stopped and smiled: "Are you OK?" "Where you be goin?" I said that I was trying to get to the 32-B bus to get home.

There was another light change as the March wind shooed a few clouds east as still more people continued to leave the building across the street, the Newton D. Baker Building, where years later I would take Calculus.

She set her bag down, looked at the # 6 bus sign that I realized was her immediate destination, lifted up her bag and then guided me across the street. It seemed clear that to get me to the bus she'd have to personally take me there, and so we both walked—south as I now know—along the street running beside Case. She told me "Case is one of the greatest Universities you could go to." This brief and knowledgeable comment by such a kindly individual made a lasting, life changing, impression on me. A very early decision, as it were.

Our walk continued towards Cedar Road which, with my shorter stride and her heavy burden, slowly came into view. Seemingly experienced, she knew how to get across this enormous highway and guide me to the 32-B sign with the large cars frantically speeding in all directions, and—for the moment—I was safe.

She smiled, lifted her bag, waving goodbye with her other hand and slowly re-crossed the street, going back to Euclid Avenue, disappearing from my view but never from my memory.

As the bus pulled up, I waved back, using the quarter she'd given to me for the fare that replaced the one I couldn't find, and I was able to find my way back home, to where I was indeed going.

Deijohnna Henderson

# November's Heart

Love is like an ocean,
It can be so dangerous,
Still you want to take a dive in,
Sorta like us women with men,
We know y'all can do us so ghastly,
Still we take our chances,
Even after you do us dirty, we still
Give passes, but to you it's different,
Your love is like the stars at
Night, so bright and beautiful you
Light my life, I ask you, what is true
To you? An uncontrollable urge to be
With someone for the rest of your
Life, you say. I said, it's like a kid
Who learns to ride a bike!! That's the
Feeling I get when I'm with you.
Your love leaves a mark, and when I
Put my head upon your chest I know
It's November's heart.

Kamilah Moore-El

# Reflection: E. 139 & Kinsman

The best days that I had were when I woke up one day and planned to go bike riding with my family and some friends. The best feeling was the breeze while riding around free having fun on a family day.

It was a nice sunny day and it was warm outside. As the day began, I went to visit my mother's house and found out that my nieces and nephews and my brothers were already revving up the mopeds, four wheelers, MB5's and Go Carts, preparing them for the road trips that we all were going to take. My younger brother helped me to put air in my tires and complete inspection.

Meanwhile my little nieces and nephews were practicing and testing their bicycles in the nearby empty parking lot located near the corner of 139th and Kinsman.

The parking lot was freshly paved and enclosed. This parking lot was the perfect place to learn how to drive almost any motor vehicle. People began to stop by while they were coming down the street. Then we had a few new riders who were coming along to ride.

After we gassed up and completed final inspections, we all grabbed a bike of choice and headed up 139th toward Byron. We began riding through the neighborhood.

We always had fun. Someone rode behind the little people and designated during the ride who would take the lead.

One limitation that we have had was that we could not ride into Shaker Heights, because we generally did not have registered bikes or even valid license plates on some of them. We were also required to wear a helmet throughout their city. One encounter that we had with Shaker Heights police ended in our bikes being confiscated and getting a ticket because Shaker was strict. In Cleveland, the police used to bother us, but now they just let us ride.

All of my family must learn how to ride at a young age. And they all must be able to recite the safety rule before riding, which is "Do Not Crash."

Rosemarie Fairman

# I know so little

I know so little of this man,
sun-capped, a child on his lap.
His eyes float above his mustache
which, if I took a crayon, I'd blush
it red. It could only be red, though
I know so little of this man.

I've been told so many things of where
he worked and how he drank. He knew
the mallet's heft and how to ring the anvil's song.
In the shipyards, his arms grew strong.
His thirst was as deep as any story,
though I know so little of this man.

He watches the children, dressed for Sunday,
as he is in sleeves bloused long and gartered,
in a shirt that sheets his chest.
A tie, a short thin spangle, is clapped to rest,
to point to the child on his lap
who'll be my father some day.

I know so little of this man
though he's as much a part of me
as Lake Erie's rain and the steel mills' soot

that blackened my father's shoes and rooted
me barely ten miles from the clapboard house
that once held this man I know so little of.

Star Anderson

# "Why I Write"

I write when I'm happy
I write when I'm sad
I write when love is new and good
I write when love turns bad
I write to express, to emote
To enlighten and to joke
I write to soar, to fly, to be free
I write 'cause to not would deny me
I write to work through
Old issues from my youth
I write for a brotha that
I want to seduce
I write 'cause I'm strong
And words have power
I write to survive my darkest hours
I write 'cause sometimes
It's how I breathe
I write the words that live inside me

# A Day in the Classroom

Wide-open Kinsman leads to dedicated students
Welcoming community spouts genuine hope
Diverse folks gather joyful days
Engaging program encourages renewed spirits
Exciting environment encourages everyone to
      learn more

Open classroom sitting round tables
Bright minds practice useful knowledge
Eager students pondering interesting opportunities
Adult learners study endless hours
Purposeful students master new skills
Curious students ask great questions
Crazy students love difficult math
Blue classroom see free people
Dedicated students generate exciting opportunities
Sophisticated students learning faster at Seeds
Proud students study continuously at
      Seeds of Literacy
Big Kev learned a lot in class
Active students learning important skills
Loyalty at Seeds is all students

Friendly student learns from helpful teachers
Dedicated tutors inspire many students
Friendly tutors value hard-working students
Energetic tutors encourage eager students
Dedicated tutors offer unique skills
Charming teachers are beautiful people
Caring site directors helping grateful students
Smart people teach others better
Comfortable class learns American English

Welcoming neighbors persist strong communities
Focused practice yields higher scores
Special friendships reward Seeds people
Fascinating facts inspire magnificent learning
Good energy motivating educational goals
From Seeds come happy graduates
Choices, it's never too late at Seeds

We are loved by the staff,
Some of us are cool with the math

# Contributors

**Star Anderson** was born and raised in Cleveland, Ohio. She began writing at the age of nine and was first published at the age of fourteen. Star is a singer, poet, spoken word artist, author, actor and model. Currently, Star has a collection of poetry as well as two novels in process. She is planning the release of her poetry collection in 2020. In anticipation Star shares some of her work and events on Instagram.

**Bob Bejdovec** was born in Cleveland and lived the first five years of his life on Aetna Road. Later, his family moved to Garfield Heights. He graduated from Benedictine High School in 1966. He served in the Army for four years which included a tour of Viet Nam. He married in 1972 and attended college and graduate school where he majored in Accounting and Business Administration. Upon retiring, Bob became a volunteer tutor at Seeds of Literacy.

**Danielle N. Dixon** is a poet, author and artist from Cleveland, Ohio, currently residing in Warrensville Heights. Danielle has competed in poetry slams across Ohio and Michigan, winning five. She currently has a CD available on Amazon.com where she has put poetry to music from her book *Sagittariusly Blunt*. Danielle's work has been published in *Inclusion Magazine* and *Luna Negra*. Danielle lived in the Glenville area until she was 14 when she and her mother moved into the family home in the Mount Pleasant area. She would later own that home and lived there until 2011. Danielle is currently working on several new writing projects that include monologues, short stories, and a memoir. She expects to release a new book of poetry in 2020. Danielle is available for bookings and can be reached on

Facebook and Instagram under Danielle Nicole Nikki Dixon.

**Rosemarie Fairman**, a native Clevelander, is a steel-belt kid who has grown into a rust-belt grandma. She writes poetry and nonfiction, teaches creative writing workshops for young adults, and assists the teen editors at Lake Erie Ink with the Teen Book Project. Fairman's present nonfiction project focuses on a family with a quadriplegic mother. Formerly, she taught literature and writing at Beaumont School in Cleveland Heights and Adult Education classes in the Greater Cleveland area. She holds a B. A. from Cleveland State University and M.Ed. in Reading from Notre Dame College.

**S. Alease Ferguson** is a scholarly researcher and practitioner in the areas of organizational health, cultural diversity, relational psychology, and African American women's mental health concerns and resistances to social oppression. To date, her solo and co-authored works have been widely anthologized in the feminist press. She has also published an edited volume with Toni C. King, titled: Black Womanist Leadership: Tracing the Motherline (SUNY Press, 2011).

**Kisha Nicole Foster** is a mother, poet, and an arts administrator. She is the author of Poems: 1999-2014 and Blood Work. Foster is the recipient of the 2019 Cleveland Arts Prize for Literature. Foster is also in her fourth year as Regional Coordinator for Poetry Out Loud, a program of The Poetry Foundation and the National Endowment of the Arts, sponsored through The Ohio Arts Council. She is a two-time Pink Door

Fellow. Foster is currently the Literary Cleveland Fellow/ Cleveland Stories program coordinator, and most recently crafted a poem for the Tamir Rice Foundation and their event "Arts, Activism, and Legacy" at the Cleveland Museum of Art. Foster uses her locution as a conduit towards healing and fostering truth within language, allowing mistakes and humility to guide her craft.

**Rose Griffin** lives in Cleveland and was married to an Army veteran. She raised four sons and decided to study for her GED at Seeds of Literacy. Last year Rose attended the Cleveland Stories workshops but did not complete a story. This year, she has become a prolific writer. At age 61, Rose has had some challenges in life but is still excited about going back to school.

**Deijohnna Henderson** was born In Pittsburgh, Pennsylvania. She attended schools there until the 10th grade, then moved to Cleveland, Ohio. She now attends Seeds of Literacy. She plans on going to college to open her own business and be an anthropologist and a chef. She would love to write her own book one day and be a public speaker to help people all around the world.

Originally from Cleveland, **Jamie Hinton** dropped out of high school to have a child. "Always wanted to be a writer so I found Seeds of Literacy in order to complete my GED so that I can become a writer."

**Lionel Johnson** was born in Cleveland in 1949 to Oscar and Juanita Johnson. He attended Cleveland Public Schools along with his brother Darryl and sister Alexis.

He later attended Cuyahoga Community College. Lionel was a participant in last year's Cleveland Stories project who found that his life was changed by the experience. His worked is filled with black vernacular that audiences enjoy. He is hard at work on finishing his first novel.

**Louis McCoy** is a writer from the Mt. Pleasant neighborhood.

**Kamilah Moore-El** grew up in Woodland Hills and moved to the Mt. Pleasant neighborhood in 1990. She is a former substitute teacher for the Cleveland Municipal School District. Currently she is a certified State Tested Nursing Assistant. She is a graduate of Cuyahoga Community College of Arts & Science and the College of Health Sciences. Kamilah was a participant in last year's Cleveland Stories and found it a life changing experience.

**Charlotte Morgan** is a writer from the Glenville neighborhood who has realized her deep ties to the Mt. Pleasant area as a result of working with the Cleveland Stories project. She teaches composition at Cleveland State University and nonfiction for Literary Cleveland. She is finishing up edits on a book-length memoir about growing up in Glenville.

**Willie Naps** is the pen name of **Will Napoli** on *The Wanted Girls*, a Hip Hop journal, and related fiction, music, comics, and poetry. "On Broadway" is a prose poem that features the HopLife style Naps uses in *The Wanted Girls* which mixes rap in the narrative when the action picks up or the narrator is ranting. The poem is part of *The Wanted Girls* series. "The Height" is also a part of *The Wanted Girls*, a preview of the first book in the series, chronologically, *The Dream Life*. It was written in class after a prompt from Kisha Foster. The second book in the series, *Hook Up*, is the first and only one published to date. An audio book edition of *Hook Up* is planned as well as music CDs featuring early home recordings of Willie Naps Jazz Band, Willie Naps Blues Band, and the Hop Shop. Artists are sought to collaborate on a graphic novel for *The Wanted Girls*, which is already written, but not yet drawn. Splendid! #4 is due out soon and will contain experimental poetry inspired by prompts from Lit Cleveland instructors as well as more fiction, journal, and flows.

**Oluremi Ann Oliver** is a writer from the Mt. Pleasant neighborhood.

**Naima Omar** was born in Atlanta, Georgia to John and Valerie who taught her how to think for herself. She moved to Cleveland at age five. She attended AJ Rickoff, Robert Fulton, Riverside and Gracemount Elementary Schools. She earned Associate degrees in specialized technology from Pennsylvania Culinary and Bryant & Stratton Colleges. Naima was also a participant in last year's Cleveland Stories project. She has two children.

**Rodney Pulley** grew up in the Buckeye area. His parents bought a home there in 1967. He attended John Adams High School, but he did not graduate. He says, "That's why I attend Seeds of Literacy. I want people to know about a part of my life that we all go through. I want to give people an insight into how the neighborhood used to be like. I want people to know there was a 'before' to our neighborhood—it was a time I enjoyed."

**Barbara Roberson** is a writer from the Mt. Pleasant neighborhood.

**Dr. Stuart Terman** lived on E. 153rd near Kinsman with his grandparents for several years. He graduated from Case Western Reserve University and then graduated from medical school in Wisconsin. He trained at the Cleveland Clinic and Michael Reese Hospital in Chicago, and was an Assistant Clinical Professor of Ophthalmology at CWRU through 2012, practicing in Solon. He has been published in numerous journals. Stuart was also a participant in last year's Cleveland Stories program. He's married and has four grown children.

A community based poet and writer, **D.L. Ware** is a literacy advocate and literary artist in Southeast Cleveland's Buckeye, Woodland Hills, and Mt. Pleasant neighborhoods. Since 2010, Ware has used his love for the literary arts as means to bring communities together. In 2015 D.L. was commissioned by Land Studio to create "Love Lunes Over Buckeye," a literary place making project that displays "Lune Poetry" on the facade of vacant buildings along Buckeye Road's upper corridor. In 2016 he was also commissioned by the Cleveland Sewer District to create "Ode to Lake Erie," a calligram poem that will be inlaid into the ground of the Sewer District's "Buckeye Green Infrastructure" project. In 2018 D.L. developed and led a weekly creative writing workshop called "Veterans' Voices," a 9-week creative writing workshop to encourage and support US Military Veterans to write and share their military experiences as a community. Husband and father of three boys, D.L. finds the act of writing to be healthy and therapeutic and makes time to write daily.

**Bernice (Niecy) Watson** was born in Cleveland, Ohio. She attended George Washington Carver Elementary School and went on to John Hay High School. She is now enrolled at Seeds of Literacy to work toward her GED. She enjoys spoken word poetry which she has been doing for six months. She wishes to touch everyone with her stories.

**Seeds of Literacy** is an award-winning nonprofit organization in Cleveland, Ohio that provides free basic education and GED®, TASC®, and HiSET® preparation to adults in the Cleveland area. Today, Seeds is serving over 900 active students with the help of approximately 250 volunteer tutors. Seeds of Literacy's Kinsman Road location, known affectionately as "Seeds East," just celebrated its 5th anniversary in September 2019. Many of the students who attend classes at this location live in the Mt. Pleasant neighborhood or surrounding neighborhoods and have contributed pieces to this anthology.

# Photo Credits

# LITERARY
## C L E V E L A N D

*Explore other voices; discover your own.*

Literary Cleveland is a community of writers committed to bringing people into the world of words by providing educational writing opportunities at all levels, promoting new and existing literature of the highest quality, and advancing Northeast Ohio as a vital center of diverse voices and visions.

To find a class or event that interests you, and to become a member, please visit our website: litcleveland.org